the length of this gap

Kristen E. Nelson

the length of this gap
Copyright © August 2018 Kristen E. Nelson

Published by Damaged Goods Press
Edited by Caseyrenée Lopez
www.damagedgoodspress.com

All rights reserved. No part or parts of this book may be reproduced in any format without the expressed written consent of Damaged Goods Press or Kristen E. Nelson.

ISBN-13: 978-0-9978267-7-7
ISBN-10: 0-9978267-7-0

Printed in the United States of America
Richmond, Virginia

Cover design by Caseyrenée Lopez
Cover photo by Julius Schlosburg
Ghosty Illustrations by Noah Saterstrom

acknowledgements

The following literary journals have published pieces from this manuscript including: *Drunken Boat*: "Ghosty", "Dinosaur Bees", "Song of Praise: Him One, Him Two, & Him Three", and "Yvette", *Everyday Genius*: "Home, Still" and *Drunken Boat*: selections from "Family Portraits."

Unthinkable Creatures Press published *Write, Dad*, a chapbook with a selection of pieces from this full-length manuscript. *The Volta* published a video project of excerpts from *Write, Dad*.

Thank you to the following people who read different versions of this book over the years, offered encouragement, and kept me afloat: Samantha Bounkeua, TC Tolbert, Frankie Rollins, Hannah Ensor, Julia Saterstrom, Jill Brammer, Erin Cox, Rebecca Brown, Bhanu Kapil, Kate Greenstreet, Logan Phillips, CA Conrad, Lily Hoang, Emji Spero, Kristen Stone, Jean Nelson, Melissa Nelson, Phyl Noto, Brian Donegan, Maggie Golston, Julianna Spallholz, Shelly Taylor, Selah Saterstrom, Kristi Maxwell, Noah Saterstrom, Kimi Eisele, Timothy Dyke, Ty Defoe, Liz Latty, and Emily Stern. Thank you to Caseyrenée Lopez and Damaged Goods Press for all of their labor to put this book into the world. Thank you to Noah Saterstrom for the Ghosty Illustrations; I could not have told that story without you. Thank you to Julius Schlosburg for the gorgeous cover photo and to TC Tolbert for conceptualizing the cover design.

*For my mother, who taught me to write it all down
and Julia, who kept me alive in all of the death.*

the length of this gap
poems hybrid prose vignettes & other liminal forms

Kristen E. Nelson

Richmond, Virginia

Just as love is an enormous field, many parts
of it have to be imagined, by everyone.

Kate Greenstreet

Contents

Silence 13
Distance 31
Anger 55
Clarity 69

about Kristen E. Nelson

Kristen E. Nelson

Silence

I have said things about you I tried not to say
but they keep asking

Kristen E. Nelson

The Length of this Gap

It begins with a hummingbird drawn in pencil:
                         my next two years

I am waiting for the day to come when her name is not beneath
                         each syllable

She sad sat there:
                         a ghost with her hard face

Her threads:
                         a ripped-up pillow case

The problem with adoration:
                         it is a little bit more than love
                         like bubbly water
                         like trying to sew the same button on
                         a pair of 3-dollar pants

I want to get smaller than those pants

What it feels like to thrust:
                         the first time
                         a barbeque
                         some over-yeasted bread
                         her, a new girlfriend, and our cat

The Length of This Gap

His body gleamed like only those who are meant for greatness do.

I look at the pale ridge inside my elbow, blue vein.

Maybe you can pretend that it's me walking away?

I can be him sometimes,
heavy and untouchable,
a composite
of all the people
I have loved
ripping out your tongue, so you can't speak

                        you feed me
                        there is no more of you

A poem is a negotiation of light and space
like a photograph of shuttered windows.

Shed layers and put your body in water.
It is the only option for survival.

I want to cover myself in all of the pendants gifted by lovers:
unicorns and wood
rose quartz and goddesses

I want to cloak myself in their protection, a cloak of gift and grieving

Your small mountain goat
is bigger than a small mountain goat on this cloak

Take cards out of box
Shuffle
Pull a card

The Queen of Wands, the most sexual of all queens
her and her black cat

Home, still

When you brought me to your home for the first time, I knew the mountains and the grandfather Saguaros. I found my ocean from the top of those mountains. I looked down and felt small. Winding roads. I was dizzy.

There is no such thing as weather; there is only heat that destroys. Quick, Easy, Moisture. I never felt mortal before this. *I am walking on the sun*, I said. You said, *Wait for the rains*. They came and smelled like sex, and I understood your love of the creosote desert. I reached for you in wet desperation. You made me wait a few more days. My city was instant gratification, but we were in your city now.

The Length of This Gap

That first time we fought, I hated you more than anyone has ever hated. I hated you more that afternoon than any other moment since. I ran to the guesthouse, sat on the floor, and tried to decide who was safe. I sucked the strength out of those old bricks. I sucked the tree roots that were destroying those old pipes into me from below. I didn't lock the door, but when you tried to come in, I held up my hand, pushed it towards you, and kept you out. A few months later when you ripped up the guesthouse carpet, it was not the mold that sicked you to the hospital.

Our neighbor, now my friend, confided
that he used to call you The Bulldog
and me The Nice One before he knew
our names. This made sense. This older
man saw some of my favorite parts of
you. Your fierceness. Your protective
nature. Your passion. Your wrinkled
forehead. Nice was all he saw of me.
You were allowed layers.

The Length of This Gap

I am traveling farther and farther away from you, Love. There is more distance now than there has ever been. I miss you is so much smaller than this. You hover over like a thunderstorm threatening. But there is comfort in the things in the sky that are loud enough to make me run for safety. The clouds and their ominous warring.

I visited you in that other house. The
one with the murals. You snuck your
small, scarred hand into mine, and I
remembered: you love me. You smelled
exactly the same, and I noticed before
you pointed that you were taking better
care of your feet. I have heard *I love
you* since that night. I have laughed at
love with parts of lovers still inside me.
She loved me the best she knew how.
He loved me the best he knew how. He
loved me the best he knew how. She
loved me the best she knew how. And
so on.

Blueprint

No mayo. No marinade. No meat. Cook green, cook yellow, cook purple. Don't eat, don't drink (too much), don't binge. No chocolate sauce. No ice-cream. No caramel. Replace sour cream and onion potato chips with wasabi almonds. Organize bowls. Organize funnels. Organize spoons. Recycle empty bottles of wine. Dump ashtray.

I wanted you here with me last night, my butter-molded butterfly. I wanted you sitting in my lap, where (our) cat sat. Can you believe he has taken to sitting on the counter tops? My long nails scratch crusty things off the bottom of the sink: healthy food bits, grains and greens, things you would never eat.

Eat in here. Hang art in here. Smoke in here. Yes, smoke in here. Chain smoke in here. Read a book and eat rainbow chard with amino acids and smoke in here. Buy a new table, place it there. Use a tablecloth, put it there. Replace the light bulbs, up there. Wash the mirror. There, there.

I make roasted eggplant and asparagus soup for dinner, and we smoke cigarette after cigarette. Smoke curled up past our fingers, past vanilla candles, past those paintings that make me so sad, past the window that will never open and up up to the high ceiling. I don't bring up your name at dinner and neither do they. I have tried hard to erase you, but you are stuck in the mold of a yet-to-be-sanded dresser, that was yet-to-be-sanded for years, that has never been stained except by whiskey, that we called the sideboard for lack of a better name.

The Length of This Gap

Keep the rug right where it is. Move the chairs around. Buy big pillows and throw them on the rug. Move in a book shelf. Move the chairs around. And again. And again. Ignore the lack of table. Ignore the lack of toys. Cover it all up, all the broken bits with an orange cloth.

The rug is covered with a sticky blanket of used white tissues and bits of used white tissues. Sometimes I lie in there and scream out, *asshole*. I play sad, sad music in there. Someday I might put my shoes in there or a pool table. There is an imprint of my body in the sticky white blanket, a pocket of sticky clouds where I lay my head. The doors are slamming over and over again from the wind, and I let them.

Hang wrought iron towel rack.
Throw away old shampoo.
Water plant. Move plant. Water plant. Move plant back to the same dusty spot.

The roaches are back. I had to chop a head off with a shampoo bottle the other morning and no one was there to hear my screaming. (Not true, not true. I silent screamed, because I didn't know if I could wake him up. I didn't want to be disappointed by him not coming to rescue me.) He scurried, I pounded. I got the willies, he ran. He paused, I caught him. He's dead now.

Throw away that fucking television. Throw away that fucking telephone with its really loud fucking ringer. Move the furniture around until the vacuum will fit between everything. Hang photos. Dust. Sit.

There is no call and response anymore. There really never was: *Marco. Marco.* But now there is no shouting, no loud-loud booming, and no shouts that weren't shouted either.

I'm not hiding anymore. I've been keeping track of things to share with you someday. Little tic marks on the walls. From far away it looks like streaks of black, but squint in closer. I've hung pictures of my family and written bold sentences in red across the walls below those pictures. Things they tell me to remember when I miss you.

Buy new sheets. Move bed up against the wall. Get rid of the un-Feng Shui mirror. Insert statue of a goddess. Insert Santa Barbara candles. Sleep.

I found that baby bird under your dresser when I moved your dresser out. I know you tried to be its birdie savior and maybe for a minute you thought it might have worked. There are things you will find out about this particular room in my house. These things are going to hurt your feelings. I think about them as rolled-up quarters.

Meadowsounds

Today from the red velvet couch, I looked out the window.

I saw couples walking with babies in strollers.

They mewed and cried and gurgled.

I went outside and hung loud wind chimes.

Distance

You saw me as beautiful
before I saw me as beautiful

The Length of this Gap

empty houses

the picturesque ruin

Mary Poppins
traded for a shadow

ghost bodies and wolves

is the difference
guided your hand
is tradition
this experience unique
money for the horse
why
didn't you expect
are your fears and the world

I'm not done waiting for you yet.

I hold my breath and see how many times I can think:

that was the day

that was the day

that was the day

The Length of This Gap

that was the day
that was the day
that was the day
that was the day

until breath
breathes my love, a wound

February eight two thousand and ten
the day my father died, the blood stopped reaching my fingers

mouth gaped open
body went still
face stopped moving
things went still
went white
went out
left the room
left the hospital
mouth gaped open
went still
fingers went numb
left the room
left the hospital
left the city

wrapped me in a heating blanket

fingers still cold

it was snowing outside

I was in my pajamas

it was snowing outside

A rip
the shape of a burial mound

That first night I was not
but you would not

let me touch you

We can risk failure
A frozen basket of onions
too cold in the pantry

Your two feet farther down
My two feet farther up
trying to stack
a pile of onions

You were 5 onions across
I am 10 onions down
four feet and ten onions
six inches and seven onions high

Distraction is an opportunity for transformation
you were never distracted
watched them roll
stacked some more

As you lay dying, Father

I am writing on the back
of my airline ticket
on my way to your hospital

I wish for many things:

>	a photo of your hand
>	a photo of your tattoo
>	a photo of your hand and its
>	tattoo it on my hand
>
>	your belt
>	buckle on my belt
>
>	you never promised
>	a happy
>
>	something
>
>	an end
>	to suffering, an end
>	to the suffering
>	you feel an end
>	to the suffering
>	I feel an end

My Father's Stories

Dear Daughter,
Merry Christmas.
Love,
Dad, Annie, and Teddy Bear

My father's wife named their dog Teddy Bear, because she collects stuffed animals. She puts the wounded ones on top of the microwave when Teddy Bear pulls off little ears and tails. My father doesn't seem to notice the microwave hospital. He picks up stuffed rabbits and cats to make room for me to sit on the couch and throws them to Teddy Bear.

I've got these boys living in my house, and they keep messing the place up. I didn't have a chance to clean. I've gotta set some ground rules with these boys.

My father lives in the middle third of a triplex in a poor neighborhood. He can't afford the rent on his pension, so he takes in boarders to cover costs. The two twenty-year old boys living there now have a dachshund. The dachshund wears a swastika collar. My father lives with dog food scattered all across the kitchen floor. His dog is overweight and so is his wife. The dachshund with the swastika is pretty fit.

Here are my family portraits.

My father's walls are decorated with palm-leaf crosses and photographs. Cross, frozen little girl, cross, frozen little girl, cross. The portraits are mass-produced Christmas cards taped to the wall. He is not in any of the portraits.

I don't know why I'm still alive. Just to drink and have a good time I think.

My father used to have curly blond hair, bright blue eyes, and killer shoulders. Now he is shrunken. His hair is short and gray. His nose is bulbous and red.

These two n_____s walk into a bar.

My father tells jokes. At the restaurant, the manager is a black man. My father glows under his complements and customer service. Then he tells more jokes. I am tempted to tell a joke about an old, wrinkled, drunk ex-cop with a fat wife who has nothing of consequence in his life, but I can't think of a punch line.

I love you.

My father does not love me.

I went to Vietnam and trained the insurgents. You have no idea what atrocities I've seen.

My father did not go to Vietnam.

Remember when I went to Alabama when your sister got sick? I'm so glad I could help take care of her.

My father went to Alabama two years before my sister was diagnosed with cancer. He got off the train with a half-empty bottle of Jack Daniels. She called me crying. I heard the sound of cartoons in the background. My father was laughing. My sister's children were not laughing.

I never had to shoot anybody when I was a cop.

When my father was drunk, and I was two years old, he tried to shoot me with his service revolver. He tried to shoot my sister and my mother. I don't know who else he tried to shoot but missed.

Come stand out on my porch and take some family portraits in front of my beautiful mountains.

My father does not know what real mountains look like. His mountains are hills covered with electrical towers. I want to take pictures of his home while he is not looking. Of the pile of dog shit on his rug, the bowed wooden floors, the smoke from his Marlboro Reds, the open pasta boxes, the cheap beer, his wife's large forehead, the dead plants, his fake Christmas tree covered in tinsel, the series of portraits of my sisters and me between crosses.

Ghosty
Illustrations by Noah Satertrom

The ending began with the Christmas card I got from you, your wife, and your dog two years ago. You were almost a ghost. Your shell was shrinking. Your wife was wide and short. You were wearing a black sweat suit and a Santa hat. Your couch covered with stuffed animals. There was a ghost coming into the picture from the left. The kind of black smudge that paranormal TV shows use as evidence. I got your message. The darkness creeping in and my last chance.

I visited you that Christmas. You cried. You invited me back last Christmas. I did not come. Your wife invited me to watch you die in February. I came.

You fell down a flight of steps. Your heart gave out. You lay there dead at the bottom of the steps until a medic brought you back. Then later in the hospital, I saw the blood in your ear, and I wanted to lick it out like a cat. My cat has a chemical burn under his ear that is always rough. Now when I rub him there, I think of you. Your body was burned. That caked blood on your face was burned.

Your wife gave me the ring you wore every day with the inscription, *Who Dares Wins*. "He wanted you to have this," she said. The words are rubbed almost illegible. I never saw your thumb rubbing over *Who* rubbing over *Dares* rubbing over *Wins*. I watched the nurse use hand lotion to pull it off your dead finger. She slipped it onto mine, still covered in lotion. I didn't take it off or wash it for days. I don't rub it, but I read it, wearing *Who Dares* down with my eyes.

The Length of This Gap

When I killed you, I wasn't there, but I tried to be. My alive sister was there. My dead sister hovered above you, always willing to wait for you. Your friends were at the foot of your bed. They were ugly, pock-marked, swollen, badly-groomed, ignorant, unkempt. Were you ever proud of me–your well-educated, n____r-loving, dyke daughter?

Your wife was by your head with doe terror. She kept repeating, "What am I going to do without him?" I never called you after you got married to tell you that your wife and mine had the same name.

They called you *Hero*, because you used to be a cop. They called you *Good Husband*, because you didn't beat your wife. They called you *Good Friend*, because you told off-color jokes.

Your wife is an idiot. When you died, I couldn't buy her flowers because you did. Once in eight years of marriage. Carnations and baby's breath in a throw-away glass vase. Your wife photographed it. She kept it on her kitchen table with the ribbon still attached after six years. She filled it with fake sunflowers.

When you died, I bought her a purple, sparkled, winged, stuffed unicorn from the Price Chopper, where she introduced me to strangers as her daughter. Once when I was 16, you took me to brunch at West Point. You introduced me as your daughter to strangers. I have only met your wife three times.

She clutched the unicorn to her chest and cried. She thanked her daughter for the present.

Your wife called me and asked me for five hundred dollars to pick up your ashes. She wants to put you on top of the TV. I didn't give her the money.

The Length of This Gap

This is how I remember you. While you were dying your wife said, "He was a cop in New York City." The assistant hospital chaplain said, "Wow, a hero." She stared at my sister and me expecting another example of a life well-lived. I could not come up with anything. My sister said, "He took up a lot of space."

Everyone in the ICU nodded as if this was a normal thing to say. A friend said, "Yes, he did have a big personality." I looked at your shrunken dying body. You used to be a big man with broad shoulders. You filled in the cracks of every love my sister and I have ever had. Your drunken voice on my answering machine last Father's Day got louder and louder. You got bigger and bigger in my heart until you popped it when I was ten. When I was a kid you were larger than life, sometimes a legend. But, you were never my hero.

I am still waiting for something to say to the chaplain. My unspoken answer fills up my mouth. It gets bigger and bigger and bigger and bigger.

Kristen E. Nelson

Anger

over-prepare and be ready
to abandon everything

The Length of this Gap

My feet are stuck wrapped up solid sinking
There is so much work to do today

Very small feet-sized coffins
There is so much work to do today

Have you ever had a near death experience?
There is so much work to do today

A moment of startle can be your guide
There is so much work to do today

The beauty of the imposed accident
There is so much work to do today

Forcing yourself into the wrong repetition
There is so much work to do today.

There is so much today.
There   is so much work to do today.

we learn to trust on release
what light will reveal
what we need
reveal yourself

                someone is screaming
                someone else asks for a cigarette
                someone else wants food
                someone cut the cord with the pain body

seeing where is my home
leave old narratives behind
pick up mine and flee the past
wake in a new towards morning

                Legba and her crossroads
                Virgin Mary energy
                a midwife to help me deliver myself
                a little villain

there are butterflies in the bedroom
a silver letter opener
I am a beach
I do not apologize

Kristen E. Nelson

I am anticipating your departure new _____

I have a body intellect much smarter than my brain

My breasts know what temporary feels like

My ears know when noises are meant to arouse and not to claim

My back knows the difference between a caress and a careless stroke

My stomach knows the difference between him and everyone else

If I had known that he was going,
I would have sacrificed too much to make him stay

The men who go away that carried me in their wallets

        Please can you tell me what a wish looks like volume
        does not begin to describe it begins
        as a two-dimensional shape shoots out
        on either side a fragile column like a switch

        that anyone can turn off

Song of Praise

Key: F

My Darling, My Love.
I don't feel you
Anywhere tonight.
I do not feel.

Refrain: No no no no no
                   no no no no no
                   no no no no:
                   no no no no no
                   no, Dear God, no.

You are simply gone.
No dreams, no church.
You are dead, simply.
No dreams, no church.

Lift, My Love, lift up.
There are no songs.
No ceremony.
Lift, My Love, lift.

Eulogy

1996

I remember that time in the rain. You were in the rain. I was sitting inside my car. I wish I could say you pulled me outside and made me laugh. I wish I could say we danced. Your romantic ideas were too storybook for me.

1997

People used to walk past us and say, *Damn*. They were talking about you. It was hard to not be the prettier one.

1998

You gave me a gold bracelet for our third anniversary. It is made out of gold hearts and gold X's. For three years, I never took it off. Sometimes I still wear it, to remember what love feels like. I run my finger over it, like you used to. I can never remember which is the kiss and which is the hug.

1999

We never had sex without kissing, even in the morning. We always smiled after we saw each other when some time had passed. It didn't matter how we parted. Your eyes glowed. You cared about my pleasure. You always wanted to sit close enough to touch me. You made me feel filled with possibility. You made me feel strong. You looked at me like you knew me. You looked at me like you wanted to know more. You wanted me to let go. You wanted to keep me safe.

2007

You sobbed in my arms. You made baby noises. You were not big and strong. You were small and hurting. You told me that women were worse than men with their catcalls. They made you feel cheap. You, who posed as the centerfold for a porn magazine. You, who flexed your stomach and wanted me to sit on you while you did push-ups. You cried. You sobbed in my arms. You talked about your mother and how cruel she could be with her insults. You trusted me, and I hope you do not know what I was thinking: *Shut up shut up shut up*. After an hour of this, you made love to me. I took all of that sadness into my body. I took those catcalls. I took those baby noises. I took your cheapness. I took those insults from your mother. I took them in from behind. I told you: *as hard as you want.*

2008

I am not a small girl, but you held me up for a long time.

2009

Sometimes there are so many big chunks of fleshy grief in your tub that you have to chip cracks in the tub itself to let in rivulets of joy. Enough to fill in the cracks between the chunks. Enough to flood the tub and float those chunks out.

2010

I found this beautiful shell at 100 feet in the Sea of Cortez, barnacle-covered, each half bigger than my palm, lined with mother of pearl. I stood in my bedroom looking at it. I placed one on my altar and thought the other half should go to you. I imagined placing it on your grave. Could I halve myself that way? You did not visit me in my dream; you did not come to say goodbye. An alive person should come before a dead person anyway. Right?

2010

You said *yo* a lot. It always made me laugh. You answered the phone, *What's good?* When they told me that you were dead I said: *No.* I said it over and over again. I could not find another word. It felt like ripping. Not a wave and not sadness. A rip in everything I had ever known. It felt unacceptable.

2010

You liked one word: lift. I liked so many. When I visit your grave, I want to take out my pocketknife. I want to dig you up and cut that tattoo out of your inner arm. Lift. I want to sew it into my own skin, to wear it on my inner arm. You said that it was an acronym for something. I don't remember what. Now it is a wish. Lift.

Yvette

To hold your hand today while all
those balloons let loose
in Wilson Woods
You know

but I wish
I was
while you let go

Yvette, I loved him.
Do you remember

I chased him
when I saw him flirt
Yvette, how he ran
and how he was right to run

Yvette, I would have cut him that day

Yvette, sometimes he put on my dress
and danced
his big ol' body in a dress

Yvette, he cried
when you pushed
your Momma down those steps

Your brother
his birthday
balloon

You know he talked about you, Yvette
He talked about beautiful
He talked about you would get out

Yvette, he got out, too
He got out

Exquisite Pain

after Sophie Calle

It was an afternoon a few months ago. I was by the pool writing. I do not remember what I was writing. It was two weeks after my sister and I traveled to Scranton, Pennsylvania to have the machines turned off on my father's comatose body. I could still smell his death. My friend walked towards me.

F is dead. I'm sorry. F is dead.

My grief was immediate. I moaned. I said, *No* over and over again. I screamed. I kept screaming. My friend held me while I screamed.

She helped me inside my house where I huddled by the toilet, puking and crying. I could not accept that he was gone. My father was gone; F was not gone. Then I got lost.

I went to a different place. I went back to several years earlier, when we prayed in the truck together. When she was still the one person who loved me enough to make things right. We prayed together in the truck. I asked her to pray with me that F wasn't dead. We held hands, and we prayed. I puked, we prayed. I was in the truck and praying.

The moment of greatest pain came when I knew that I could not stay in the truck.

Song of Praise

Key: J

My Friend, your stories
never made sense.
My Friend, Unicorn
should have rotted

Refrain: You told a story
                of a unicorn
                His horn was gone
                he should have rotted
                not you, not you

He was saved by love
You died outside
He was fed and lived
You died outside

You were twenty-nine
five days outside
Dead whiskey-soaked you
five days outside

Letters

Dearly Beloved,

You are near,
coming closer.

I mean, you were on an airplane.
It landed.

You make common movestakes:
Close then away.

You like my house, body, comfort.
You call this friendship, but you are only taking.

Friend,
then

If you ask for it,
I would give it.

Anything.
I mean, everything.

•••

Dearly Needed,

I know what it feels like.
It hurts.

Someone in this bed understands you
more than you think.

I would like to compare heart notes.
I like your body, your comfort. I am only taking.

I will not ask you for anything.
I mean, everything.

•••

This is where the closings should come.
Love and love with some commas.

Blood

Of you and you and me
I am the smallest part
No matter how you look at it

At least we form a recognizable shape

You both stand up
Lean into one another
with your arms raised
I lay on the floor between you

We are acrobats

If I call out
because someone
is stepping on my hair
one of you will hear me
and one of you will be too involved
in holding his position

If there was blood
one of you would complement
my commitment
to the shape we make

I would like to curl
I would like to stand up
I would like to walk away

Please do not walk away

You are the sum of all my parts
That doesn't make any sense
But one of you will pretend to understand it

Fasting

I pull this bow back taut

This is what holding
back looks like

Do you notice
my warped shape?

This table has been cracked
for a long time
but I still use it
It still works

Kristen E. Nelson

Clarity

an orange dragonfly swoops
a familiar arc

The Length of this Gap

She thinks in badger and in rose. She thinks here is pink and white. She stays right there for as long as she can. Then she moves on to a moment of lifting. The pilot thinks how typical the clouds look today. She thinks how the girl on the ground must look, looking up at clouds. She thinks of picking up mica from rocky paths back home. She thinks of home and how the girl will not be there and of how she can pick up mica and send the slivered pieces to the girl on the ground. The girl on the ground thinks looking up at clouds.

I didn't want to let go until we both fell into sleepy puddles on the floor and your plane was long gone and the security guard the one who kept glaring at us would have to use his toe to nudge us awake

Yes
that's right
she is not
Yes
she is not at hand

I have stored her

I have kept
little still

there is a medicine
of hands digging
in her scalp

And still
I am the best of her light

You have begged
for her light
unfold her light

she still blossoms
still divine for light

she is under
rings until dawn

SCENE 1:   Highway by moonlight in the heart of the mountains.

GIRL 1:   The colors are bright and I see that. I am curious what the other colors are. What are the blacks, dark blues, ruby reds?

GIRL 2:   Black—I prefer no torch at night, because then I am a part of the darkness

            Dark Blue—Would love, would heart, would color, would come, would halt, would run, would cry, would break, would leap, would hurt, would disappoint

            Ruby Red—I stick my finger inside of myself and pull out blood. I use that blood to write your name on my rooftop during a meteor shower. You name has several letters in my name. I write my name crisscrossing yours through the letter I. There is blood under my nail, in the crevices of my knuckles, on the fingers that rubbed up against the one that went inside.

SCENE 2:   The leaf-entombed brutal monster is colorless.

The mean fat girl has layers under her clothes

50 pounds over
a layer of fear over
a layer of shame over
a layer of ugly over
a layer of protection over
cotton underclothes

Distance [ˈdɪstəns]: the length of this gap

Silence [ˈsaɪləns]: refusal or failure to speak out

Anger [ˈæŋgə]: grief; to strangle, to float

Clarity [ˈklærɪtɪ]: clearness, brightness, splendor

My love
I dream
                      you are writing me into
                      existence

Do not bring water

I wake to lilies
their wild scent in big pink pushes spreading
shouting all of the heart wide open goofy dew

In this moment I am entirely alone

Hate

You ask your most recent beloved, *Why not?*
and he smiles and says, *You are floating.*

You realize in that moment, he knows you better than you know yourself
and that is for now how it is supposed to be.

You love him more for his knowing
and while you are exploding, he asks you, *Do you hate me?*

From *Write, Dad*

I know you
and it sucks
but with time
you have great support

no mistakes
it'll hurt
and then you'll be filled

Even in Winter

Someday I would like to say to a lover,
Do you remember the day we met?

The answer will be
a long time ago

What is left after a year

Three home movies. Expired zinc lozenges. A laser level. Foot crack cream. Country berry air freshener. An empty bottle of Tums. A bag of jingle bells. Several tags from size 18 pants. A film canister. One dime. Two match books. A bag of beads marked 2 dollars. A pre-moistened lens cleaning cloth. A receipt from Blockbuster, 2004. Expired arnica gel. A high-heeled doll foot. Expired Day-Quil. A spool of white twine. A shoe-polishing brush. A playing card. A butterfly-covered nail file. Five black pens. Four safety pins. That broken spring from the couch. A sticker that says *No Rules*.

You are still calling me. I am still calling you. My other reality still has you in it. There is still an Airstream. There is still an ocean. We sit still and make beaded jewelry for tourists. Our towheaded children still run naked in the sand. I still imagine there.

We still talk about your girlfriend. You are still saying good-bye. I think of reaching out to grab your still hand beside me in bed. I think about how your hand found my still face. I still think about how right it felt. I still hate her for cheating on you.

The Length of This Gap

I still have your note. I sit still reading you thanking me for being a good friend. I still have dreams about you. I still have not told our married friends about it. I still have not told your ex-girlfriend about it. She is still married. She is still pregnant. I am still grateful for the condom we used. I still hope my ex-girlfriend never finds out. I still think it was one of the best weekends of my life.

Still I know that your kid keeps you in a different city. Still I know that this is my city. Still I have hopes with you in them. There is still an Airstream.

I know your love is Monopoly money. You know I will dress you up in SCUBA gear. I know where you stash your coke. You know how much I need to feel beautiful. I know you want to die and how you plan to do it. You know how much living I want to do and how I plan to do it. I know the notes you write all in CAPS are not actually poems. You know the night before I left for New Orleans was not actually our last. I know the sound of beads clicking on your wrist. You know the sound of this NOLA brass band.

The Length of This Gap

A loss of hope. A box of 300 cookies. A question *why didn't I say stay?* A neti pot at your suggestion. A desire and I shake. A hand above me. A story I had to ask. A taste of new tattoo. A hike, you urging me through swarming wasps. A wish to go back and walk through wasps. A head tilt while you fed me. A not showing up when it was important. A record player that used to hiss. A seed-lady from Mexico. A prayer to St. Francis.

about Kristen E. Nelson

photo credit Julius Schlosburg

Kristen E. Nelson is a queer writer and performer, literary activist, LGBTQ+ activist, and community builder. She is the author of *the length of this gap* (Damaged Goods, August 2018) and two chapbooks: *sometimes I gets lost and is grateful for noises in the dark* (Dancing Girl, 2017) and *Write, Dad* (Unthinkable Creatures, 2012). Kristen's poem "After the Crotalus atrox" was anthologized in *The Sonoran Desert: A Literary Field Guide* and nominated for a 2016 Pushcart Prize by University of Arizona Press. She has published work in *Bombay Gin*, *Denver Quarterly*, *Drunken Boat*, *Tarpaulin Sky Journal*, *Trickhouse*, and *Everyday Genius*, among others. Kristen shares her work frequently at venues across the United States as a featured performer for events such as the *Trickhouse Journal* launch at New York's Bowery Poetry Club, as an opening act for singer/songwriter Dar Williams at Tucson's Rialto Theater, and as a keynote performer at LA's Open Press Conference.

Find Kristen online at www.kristenenelson.com.

Made in the USA
Columbia, SC
14 October 2018